YURY BALANENKO · ALEXANDER BEREZIN

MOSCOW

PLANETA PUBLISHERS ⋒ MOSCOW

Editor
YURY BALANENKO

Design
DMITRY BISTI

Colour photography
NIKOLAI RAKHMANOV

The Union of Soviet Socialist Republics and the Soviet Communist Party constitute Lenin's priceless legacy to mankind.

It was Lenin who created the Party, led it through three revolutions to the helm of government, and headed the world's first socialist state. Lenin's genius made it possible for Soviet Russia and the rest of humanity to enter a new historical era.

"So vast was the scope of Lenin's thinking and activity, so fully did he understand and express the urgent needs of his time, that even now his ideas are a mighty weapon in the hands of those who are struggling for the happiness of peoples. There is not a spot on earth where Lenin's name does not resound as an ardent call to fight oppression, lawlessness and exploitation; everywhere his name stands for militant unity and assurance of victory in the historic battle for communist ideals" — said Leonid Brezhnev in his report on the occasion of Lenin's centenary.

Lenin has played an enormous part in Moscow's development, setting in motion a new series of events.

Many centuries went into the development of Moscow. Primitive communes of remote ancestors of the Slavs existed on the site of our capital city as far back as the Neolithic period. Remains of such communes dating back 5,000 years have been found in the vicinity of Lyalovo Village on the Klyazma River and in the city itself in Shchukino district.

A well-fortified settlement of the Iron Age has been discovered near the village of Dyakovo on the Moskva River. Dyakovo-type strongholds dating from the 7th century B.C. to the 7th century A.D. have also been found in the Potylikha district of Moscow, on Lenin Hills in the neighbourhood of the Andreyev Streets, and at Nizhniye Kotly. The territory of the Kremlin has also yielded traces of that type of civilization.

A study of ancient objects and burial rites indicates that later Dyakovo-type strongholds belonged to Slav tribes. Excavations show the course of development from the Dyakovo period to the time of the Old Russian Chronicles. In the Tver Chronicles of 1147 it was recorded that Prince Yury Dolgoruky "laid the corner-stone of Moscow near the mouth of the Neglinnaya River above the River Yauza". This is the first time Moscow is mentioned in the Chronicles. Long before, however, there was an artisan settlement on Borovitsky Hill. It has been established that in 1080 the settlement had a wood-paved street with a stockade running alongside.

The Kremlin with its wooden walls and towers, situated on a hill and encircled by the Moskva and Neglinnaya rivers, became an important strategic point. Moscow stood at the juncture of land and water trade-routes. The town expanded with every year, drawing more and more artisans and tradesmen, who sought protection within its fortified walls. Surrounded by dense woods, the hill settlement was convenient both as living quarters and a defence post.

Unique objects produced by the craftsmen of old Russia which were found during excavations are on display at the museums of the Kremlin and at the History Museum, and we can only marvel at the high degree of craftsmanship achieved by the stone-masons, the goldsmiths, the wood-carvers at the beautifully finished wordk on leather.

In the fourteenth century Moscow became the capital of Russia's strongest principality, one of its biggest towns, a centre for trades and handicrafts. The local gunsmiths, blacksmiths, casters of cannon and bells, were well known for the excellent quality of their work. The occupation of the people of the time is still evident in the old names of Moscow's streets and lanes, squares and embankments. There are Pushechnaya (Cannon Makers) and Bronnaya (Gunsmith) Streets, Taganskaya (Iron-mongers) Square, Ruzheiny (Armoury) and Runovsky (Weavers') Lanes.

When almost all the Russian principalities united around Moscow, it grew into a force capable of shaking off the Tartar yoke which Russia had borne for more than 200 years and of repulsing the Lithuanian invasion.

After freeing itself, Moscow in the fifteenth century became the economic and political capital of the vast Russian state on the eastern borders of Europe.

Moscow soon developed into the cultural centre of all of Russia. The finest craftsmen flocked to the capital from Pskov, Rostov the Great, Vladimir. As a result splendid buildings arose in the Kremlin in place of the palaces which had become old and shabby. Architects from Italy also arrived to take part in the work. It is fortunate that none of the construction or reconstruction projects ever violated the artistic harmony and unity of the Kremlin ensemble. The additions simply contributed new features emphasizing the incomparable, distinctive style of the period. The Kremlin is an example of the old Russian classic style inspired by the traditions of Moscow, Novgorod-Pskov, and Vladimir-Suzdal architecture with its simple lines, harmonious colours, supple grace and monumentality.

In the sixteenth century Moscow was already one of the largest towns in Europe. Foreign visitors used to say that it was bigger than London, Prague or Florence. The Kremlin had become the administrative centre of the Russian capital. A number of magnificent examples of the architecture of the time have come down to us. They include the Bell Tower of Ivan the Great, St Basil's Cathedral, and the Annunciation Cathedral at the Kremlin in its present aspect.

The formation of a multi-national centralized state was accompanied by the development of an all-Russian literature, the art of printing and the book trade.

The sixteenth century marked the beginnings of opposition to the feudal-serf system. With internecine warfare, the constant threat of foreign invasion, poor grain crops, and ruinous taxation the discontent of the people in June 1547 flared into open revolt. The uprising was savagely suppressed, but it forced Russi's ruling class and the recently enthroned Ivan the Fourth, who subsequently became known as Ivan the Terrible, to take decisive measures to strengthen centralized rule.

A terrible disaster struck Moscow in 1571 when the armies of Khan Devlet-Girei of the Crimea burned down the capital city. However, the Khan's second attempt to break through Moscow's defences failed.

Exploitation of the people by serf-owners stiffened, class contradictions grew, and popular movements arose repeatedly in Russia and endured for a long period.

The struggle of the enslaved peasantry intensified by the hungry years of 1601 and 1603, by dissension among the *boyars,* and by the Polish and Lithuanian invasions broke out into actual war against feudal oppression. The two-months siege of Moscow by the Peasant Army led by Ivan Bolotnikov, who had the sympathy of the artisans and *kholops* (serfs), dealt a severe blow to the serf system. The insurrection lasted from June, 1606, to October, 1607. As the years passed the Russian state grew stronger, its cultural life expanded, but the lot of the common people was still hard. In Moscow's Red Square the Tzar's decrees were read from the *Lobnoye Mesto,* and the rebellious were executed there. Stepan Razin, the people's hero who had fought against tyranny, was quartered there in June, 1671. In January, 1775 a large crowd watched the execution of Emelyan Pugachov, leader of the Great Peasant War, on Bolotnaya Square. The rumble of popular unrest resounded in Moscow before and after these events. The townspeople revolted in 1648 and in 1662, the *streltsi* (the Tzar's bodyguard) in 1682 and 1698.

But even under serfdom folk art flourished. The craftsmen of the time have left us architectural monuments remarkable for their grace, balance of form, intricate carving on white stone, beauty of decorative design. We are also charmed by the elegance of the interior decoration.

The latter half of the seventeenth century witnessed advances in education. More and more of Moscow's inhabitants were learning to read and write. There was a growing demand for translated literature. Books published in Kiev and Chernigov appeared in the shops in Russian and other Slavic languages. In 1665 a school was opened at the Zaikonospassky Monastery in Nikolskaya Street, with Simeon Polotsky, prominent Byelorussian poet and scholar, at the head of it. Later a school was set up at the Printing House. It taught Latin, Greek and Slavic to pupils from various classes of the population. A school of Slavic, Greek and Latin, known as the Academy, was opened under the sponsorship of Simeon Polotsky in 1687. It was to be connected with men such as Antiokh Kantemir, Vassily Trediakovsky and Mikhail Lomonosov. To the latter, a brilliant scholar of lowly origin but great natural gifts, Moscow is indebted for founding in 1755 Moscow University, which has played a big part in the development of Russian science and culture.

Moscow's two architectural museums, one at the former Donskoy Monastery and the other in Kalinin Prospekt, demonstrate that Moscow architects of the seventeenth century and later, seeking a fresh approach in European Renaissance, Baroque and classic architecture, often found their own style of expressing the age-old traditions of Russian culture.

Dmitry Ukhtomsky, a prominent architect of the mid-seventeen hundreds, was known as an excellent teacher as well as a designer of buildings. The two famous architects Vassily Bazhenov and Matvei Kazakov developed under his tutorship.

The nineteenth century was dramatically ushered in by the flames of war. Napoleon's armies, 600,000 strong, after marching across Western Europe, invaded Russia on the night of June 12, 1812.

The 34 monuments at Borodino Field on the approaches to Moscow are the silent, but formidable witnesses of Russian martial glory of the Patriotic War of 1812. Among them are the Fortifications of General Bagration, the Shevardino Redoubt, the Monument of Field-Marshal Kutuzov. They stand like motionless guards at points where the fighting was heaviest...

Some 130 years later Borodino was again to become a battle field in the war against nazi Germany.

The past lives again in expositions at the History Museum, the Borodino Museum, "The Battle of Borodino" Panorama-Museum. The celebrated Arch of Triumph designed by Osip Bove has been reconstructed on Kutuzov Prospekt in honour of the victory of the Russian people over Napoleon's army.

Moscow was in flames during the French invasion. Fortunately the Kremlin as a whole did not burn down, but the Belfry, Metropolitan Filaret's Extension, the Bell Tower of Ivan the Great, the Arsenal and a number of towers were damaged. In the city itself two thirds of the houses were destroyed by the fire. Peter the First had ordered that only stone buildings were to go up in Moscow, but after he moved the capital to St Petersburg, people went back to the old way and wooden construction was again prevalent in Moscow.

Soon after the end of the Napoleonic War the city began to rise from the ruins. A special commission for the reconstruction of Moscow was set up headed by Osip Bove, a leading Russian architect and pupil of Matvei Kazakov. Bove took part in designing the Bolshoi Theatre and the ensemble on the adjacent square. He also directed the landscaping of the Alexandrov Gardens and designed the Grotto at the Middle Arsenal Tower.

Dementy Gilardi, another pupil of Kazakov, has a prominent place in the history of Moscow architecture. Like Bove he was engaged in reconstruction work after the Moscow fire of 1812. His style is distinguished by expressive, austere lines. Each of his creations contributed something new in architectural design. In reconstructing Moscow University Gilardi in the main followed Kazakov's original plan and specifications, but he changed the central part of the façade; the Assembly Hall, which had to be entirely rebuilt, became even more stately.

The development of Moscow architecture came to a halt in the latter part of the nineteenth and the beginning of the twentieth centuries. Buildings were being put up mainly for profit without regard to beauty or harmony. Next to the pretentious homes of manufacturers stood the modest dwellings of government officials and the tiny huts of the artisan population. With the high cost of land there was no space whatever between buildings. It often happened that an ostentatious mansion to suit the vulgar taste of a newly-rich merchant would be flanked by some priceless seventeenth or eighteenth-century monument. On the other hand it might be rubbing shoulders with a tumble-down shack. On the outskirts of the town more and more barracks were going up for the working people. The style of the better residences was a mixture of various schools and trends. There was not a trace of old Russian architecture or the traditions of the eighteenth century.

The Soviet capital today with its dynamic rhythm of life and rapid advance is the result of the October Socialist

Revolution and the revolution in science and technology that followed it.

It was only after the Revolution that Moscow's architects began planning the long-term reconstruction of the city. Moscow, with its rich cultural inheritance, not only cherished the architectural monuments of the past, but gave them new meaning. It is the harmonious blend of old traditions with the new that gives the Soviet capital its distinctive, incomparable aspect.

Over the past ten years Moscow has expanded two and a half times. Today it covers an area of 87,000 hectares. It is bigger than New York with its 12 million population, two and a half times bigger than London, eight times than Paris. A circular highway cut through wooded areas surrounds the city. The new districts are attractive and self-sufficient. The distinguishing feature of Soviet town planning is the absence of contrast between a splendid centre and slums, which still exists in the big capitalist cities. Present-day Moscow is a city without outskirts.

Lenin played a most important part in Moscow's transformation. Measured against the age-old history of the city, his life there lasted but an instant — 100 days prior to the Revolution, counting his occasional visits, and 6 years since March, 1918, when he lived and worked there. But without that brief period Moscow as it is today would have been inconceivable. There would not be the sense of continuity between the centuries nor the fundamental features of life in a socialist city, the features which make our capital so different from the capitals of other countries. Lenin's brilliant mind and the triumph of the Revolution led by the Bolshevik Party, which was created and steeled by Lenin, made it possible for Russia, in fact for the whole world, to advance toward a new historical era.

On February 26, 1918, during the anxious time following the Revolution, when enemies were closing in on the young Soviet Republic, Lenin submitted to the Council of Peoples' Commissars the text of a decree proposing Moscow as the new capital. There was every reason for the change. It was not only that Petrograd was menaced by the German advance. The people had always regarded Moscow as the first city in the land. Russia's economic life had centred around Moscow since olden times. Moscow had often led the struggle against foreign invasion. As a big industrial centre, Moscow had an organized working class which rose up in arms during the first Russian Revolution of 1905. On December 30, 1922, when the First All-Union Congress of Soviets adopted the Declaration on the Formation of the Union of Soviet Socialist Republics, it was agreed that Moscow was to be the capital of the whole country. In Moscow the Soviet government took immediate steps to get rid of all the doss houses and barracks with their tiers of plank beds occupied by workers' families. On Lenin's proposal the inhabitants of such places and of hovels and damp, malodorous basements were moved into houses formerly owned by the bourgeoisie. The mansions of the nobility and merchants were transformed into workers' clubs and cultural centres, polyclinics and kindergartens, libraries and museums.

In the difficult years of the Civil War Moscow's population suffered from cold and hunger. All available resources were used to defend the gains of the Revolution from foreign intervention forces and internal counter-revolutionaries. Yet Lenin, the leader of the Revolution was already thinking about the reconstruction of Moscow, visualising it as a splendid socialist city.

On Lenin's initiative, architects began working on a plan to improve and beautify Moscow. Lenin was concerned with the needs of the ordinary man. He supported proposals for a housing development on the South-West side of town in the vicinity of Vorobyovy Hills. He devoted much attention to the planting of trees and shrubs, the municipal economy, the construction of an underground transport system.

Lenin insisted that during the work of reconstruction monuments of ancient architecture and all valuable examples of Russian folk art should be carefully preserved.

On the very next day after March 12, 1918, when the seat of the Soviet government was moved from Petrograd to Moscow, Lenin made a tour of the Kremlin and pointed to the need of restoring a number of its monuments and of clearing and improving the grounds. The Kremlin had been neglected since Peter's time and was badly in need of attention. The frescoes and images on the icons of old churches were almost obliterated. At Lenin's suggestion a Restoration Committee was set up. Lenin himself inspected the grounds, the cathedrals, Armoury and towers. Twice he visited the Patriarch's Sacristy and Library. He came a number of times to the Dormition Cathedral to watch the work of old masters emerging underneath more recent layers. In May, 1918 Lenin instructed that the Vladimirsky (Nikolsky) Gates be restored without delay and the Kremlin Chimes repaired. The Chimes had been hit by a shell in the fighting during the Revolution. St Basil's Cathedral that "song imprinted in stone", was also being restored on Lenin's insistence.

On October 5, 1918 a country-wide listing was started of all objects of historic and artistic value. Here is part of the text of the decree issued by the Council of Peoples' Commissars on this matter: "in order to preserve, study and make accessible to the general public art objects and treasures of the past found in Russia, the Council of Peoples' Commissars decrees that all objects of art and antiquity, whether in the form of collections or separate articles, must be listed in this first state registration regardless of ownership".

With every era making its own contribution to national and world culture, it follows that methods of city planning should change and that these changes be reflected in architecture.

We still have a good many examples of houses erected during the first ten years of Soviet government. The simple lines of the four and five-storey houses were dictated by expediency; they did not strive for a decorative effect. Although they lacked the conveniences that came later — gas, hot water, garbage disposal — they marked a new trend in housing construction. In the small flats every room had plenty of sunlight, since most of the buildings were oriented north to south. The trees and shrubs planted in the new districts were part of the general architectural scheme.

Public buildings also had a distinctive appearance. Soviet architects tried to meet the requirements of the time; their efforts left an imprint in the history of town construction. The Cultural Centre of the Likhachov Motor Car Works designed by the Vesnin brothers is an impressive example of a worker's club ensemble.

Some of the earlier buildings worthy of notice are the *Zuyev* Workers' Clubhouse, designed by Ilya Golosov, the Clubhouse for the *Kauchuk* (Rubber) Plant and the *Rusakov* Clubhouse designed by Konstantin Melnikov.

In the second half of the 1920's more new buildings appeared in Moscow — the Publishing House and Print Shop of the newspaper *Izvestia,* the Institute of Marxism-Leninism in Sovetskaya Square, the Central Telegraph Building on Gorky Street, and the Planetarium. The style in all of them is austere, perhaps a trifle cold, without exterior or interior ornamentation. Space was put to the most practical use. The chief building materials were concrete, iron and glass. Even at that time, however, the city planners were outlining the future contours of Moscow.

The country was experiencing an upsurge in industrial and cultural development. Moscow was building new plants and factories, research institutes, laboratories, educational establishments, theatres, museums and stadiums. With the rapid increase in population it was necessary to build many more homes and hotels. Streets and squares required fundamental reconstruction.

In June 1931, the Central Committee of the Communist Party, after studying the problems of Moscow's municipal economy, laid down the basic provisions of a plan for the reconstruction of Moscow, the socialist capital of a proletarian state. A decision was made to build the *Moskva-Volga* Canal (now called the *Moskva* Canal) and an Underground Transport System. Architects started work on a General Plan for Moscow's reconstruction. This plan, endorsed in June, 1935, was the first historical document to outline the main principles of socialist city planning. The document stated that the Central Committee of the Communist Party and the Council of Peoples' Commissars had rejected projects to preserve Moscow as an ancient monument and a Museum City, and to erect a new city beyond its boundaries. The Party and government had also rejected proposals to dismantle the city and to build another in its place according to an entirely different plan. Instead it was decided that the historical outlines of the city should be preserved, but that its streets and

squares should be radically reconstructed. It was of utmost importance, the document pointed out, to plan correctly the location of residential districts, industrial enterprises, railway transport and warehouses, and water supply works. Residential districts must have plenty of space between buildings. Normal, healthy conditions must be provided for the population. There must also be a uniform plan for the landscape architecture of squares, thoroughfares, embankments and parks throughout the city. Residential and public buildings should be modelled on the finest examples of classic and modern architecture and the most up-to-date methods used in constructing them.

Moscow's reconstruction plan provided for the expansion of a road system of concentric circles and spokes, more green belts, a better water supply system, and other improvements. Details of the plan with additions and corrections were worked out in the next few years. As a result of intensive efforts in the reconstruction of streets and squares, improvements in the city's utilities and communal services, Moscow was growing into a genuine socialist city.

The broad expanse of Marx Avenue took the place of the old Okhotny Ryad, with two new buildings located there — the Hotel *Moskva* designed by Alexei Shchusev and the House of the USSR Council of Ministers designed by Langman. Gorky Street (formerly Tverskaya) is now an attractive modern thoroughfare. It was straightened and broadened to two and a half times its former width. Some of the historic buildings were set back from the street. One of the structures of the former Savvinsky Monastery was transported to a new place. The Moscow Soviet was moved back 14 metres and two more storeys added to it. The Eye Clinic was turned half way around and now faces Sadovskikh Lane instead of Gorky Street.

Much has been done to improve the squares — Dzerzhinsky, Sovetskaya, Novaya and Staraya, Smolenskaya, Revolution, Sverdlov and Kommuny — as well as Teatralny Lane and Mokhovaya Street. The newly formed Manezhnaya Square (renamed the 50th Anniversary of the Revolution) now provides a view of the Alexandrov Gardens, Mokhovaya, Herzen and Gorky Streets, Revolution Square and the Manege building, the latter a splendid example of nineteenth-century Russian classic architecture.

The first Underground line went into operation in May, 1935. Two years later the *Moskva* Canal began functioning. It meant a radical improvement in the city's water supply. Moscow has become a port of five seas.

The following years saw big park projects under way, the construction of more and more cultural and public service establishments, and housing development on an ever greater scale. Moscow's appearance was enhanced by new buildings such as the Lenin Library, the Soviet Army Theatre, the Frunze Academy, the Dynamo Stadium, the Tchaikovsky Concert Hall and the River Terminal at Khimki. All these went up on the site of newly-formed squares and avenues.

The war imposed on the Soviet Union by nazi Germany put a stop to such intensive building activities for a long time to come.

It was not until the first postwar Five-Year-Plan was launched that Moscow started the job of restoring its housing fund and communal services. This was followed by a far-flung programme to build pre-fabricated homes, cultural and communal facilities. In 1951 the Soviet government endorsed a ten-year plan for Moscow's reconstruction based on the first General Plan. Before long a strong industrial base was set up. Large new housing developments were started on the Peschanaya streets, in the South-Western part of the city, Cheryomushki, Fili-Mazilovo, Khoroshevo-Mnevniki, and Izmailovo. The Lenin Stadium, a sports complex of massive proportions, arose at Luzhniki. The contours of the Kremlin were now linked with the tall apartment houses and administration buildings in Smolenskaya, Vosstaniya, and Lermontov squares, the Kotelnicheskaya Embankment, the Hotel *Ukraina* on Kutuzovsky Avenue, Hotel *Leningradskaya* on Komsomolskaya Square, and Moscow University on Lenin Hills.

In 1960 the Council of Ministers called for a new long-term General Plan to be drawn up, and in August of the same year the Supreme Soviet of the Russian Federation adopted a decree to extend Moscow's area. Now the 109-kilometre Circular Highway marks the city limits. Construction projects were started in Degunino, Zyuzino, Lenino-Dachnoye, Khimki-Khovrino, and Nagatino. New bridges, over-passes and tunnels appeared on the Sadovoye Circle, also a three-level traffic intersection on the square in front of Savelovsky Railway Station. Many underpasses were built for pedestrians.

Moscow's aspect has changed beyond recognition. In Soviet times it acquired a housing area of 90 million square metres. More than 4 million Muscovites moved into new modern flats just in the past ten years. Unique structures went up, such as the Mutual Economic Assistance Council Building, the Children's Recreation Centre on Lenin Hills, the Television Centre with its 533-metre Tower at Ostankino, the Hotel *Rossia,* the *Hydroproject* Building, and the Central Airport. Kalinin Prospekt is an outstanding example of modern city-planning.

The Kremlin now looks more beautiful than ever. It is the residence of the Soviet government, the place where the Supreme Soviets of the USSR and of the Russian Federation meet and where the USSR Council of Ministers is housed.

All the Kremlin's historical, cultural and architectural monuments are under state protection. They are carefully maintained, with restoration work going on continuously. Five Kremlin towers — Borovitskaya, Vodovzvodnaya, Spasskaya, Nikolskaya, and Troitskaya have been crowned with ruby stars. These glowing ornaments symbolize the new Moscow.

At the end of World War II restoration work began on the Kremlin walls and towers, on the Dormition, Annunciation, and Archangel Michael cathedrals, the Twelve Apostles Church, palaces and other monuments. Cathedral Square acquired a new flooring; the freshly gilded dome of the Bell Tower of Ivan the Great and the gilded cupolas of the Annunciation Cathedral shone more brilliantly than ever.

In 1961 the Palace of Congresses was added to the Kremlin ensemble. It is a fine example of modern monumental architecture. Its designers made every effort to fit it into the general architectural scheme of the Kremlin, and its austere, stately lines and beautiful interior decoration are a tribute to Soviet architecture. There are over 800 rooms, but the auditorium, which accommodates 6,000, is the largest in the world and has the finest technical equipment. The world's largest stage is separated from the auditorium by a decorative metallic curtain in the centre of which a bas-relief portrait of Lenin glows on the background of a red banner. The last word in electronic equipment assures excellent acoustics and allows the audience to hear transmissions in 29 languages.

The Kremlin Palace of Congresses is known throughout the world as the gathering place for international forums and festivals as well as for Soviet Communist Party Congresses. Representatives of all the Soviet republics and nationalities meet there to discuss administrative and social problems.

When Leonid Brezhnev reported to the 24th Communist Party Congress of the USSR, he presented even more attractive plans for Moscow's future. "Moscow", he said "is cherished by all Soviet people as the capital of our country, our biggest industrial, cultural and scientific centre, as the symbol of our great socialist state. Large-scale work in the field of housing development, town improvement and the improvement of transport facilities will continue in Moscow as before. To make Moscow a model communist city is the bounden duty of the entire Soviet people".

Lenin's dream is coming true... In June, 1971, a new General Plan, a scientifically based programme for Moscow's improvement, was adopted. The decree issued by the Central Committee of the Communist Party and USSR Council of Ministers points out that the time has come to carry out the next phase of Moscow's development, and in accordance with the General Plan, with the use of the latest achievements of Soviet and foreign science, technology and architecture, to make the Soviet capital a model communist city, a well-built modern community with all the amenities, healthful hygienic living conditions, and a well-organized system of trade, public utilities and services.

The care lavished by the Party on Moscow reflects the main principle underlying all its activities: everything is for the sake of man, everything for his benefit. Brezhnev stressed that the new General Plan strives to fulfill Lenin's bequest: "Moscow must be rebuilt so that it may become a city well planned aesthetically and convenient for the inhabitant". Making Moscow a model communist city involves more than construction and reconstruction of streets and squares, boulevards and architectural ensembles, more than giving people better services. It calls for the re-equipment of factories, the further specialization of Moscow's industries which require highly qualified labour. The capital's industrial establishments should serve as a kind of laboratory for the country providing an example of faultless production techniques, top quality output, and the highest possible productivity. Moscow must also provide an example of how to cope with social and town planning problems which invariably accompany the development of big modern cities.

Large-scale housing construction is to continue. The target for the current Ninth Five-Year-Plan (1971-1975) is an additional 18,500,000 square metres of living space, more new-type schools, hospitals, canteens, restaurants, cafés and other public service establishments. The plan calls for four times as many hotels and more sports facilities. Large sports complexes are under construction at Izmailovo, Nagatino, Krylatskoye, and on Leningradsky Avenue. A sports palace accommodating 40,000 is to go up near the Soviet Army Theatre. The apartment houses, with few exceptions, are to be nine to sixteen storeys high.

A new feature for Moscow will be its division into eight zones. One of them will incorporate the traditional part inside the Sadovoye Circle with the Kremlin as the principal architectural structure. The other seven will cluster around it. Each zone will have its own centre consisting of squares, and architectural ensembles with theatres or stadiums, parks, hotels and restaurants. This kind of pattern opens up possibilities for each zone to broaden its business and social life, to provide its inhabitants with public service establishments, work, recreation, and opportunities to engage in sports activities. A ramified city transport system will assure a minimum of time spent in travelling from home to place of employment. Highways will link the central part of all the zones with the heart of the city which will remain the principal cultural, social and administrative centre and retain its historical significance.

Two more circular roads are planned between the Sadovoye Circle and the Moscow Circular Highway. There will also be a network of expressways which will by-pass the centre of town.

The planting of trees and shrubs is an important part of Moscow's city planning. Gardens and parkways, the green areas of housing developments will reach out toward the principal parks and forested regions bringing the total planted area up to some 30 square metres per person.

The General Plan envisages the completion of park projects along the embankments, the cleaning of lakes and ponds and the creation of new reservoirs.

At present the daily per capita consumption of water in Moscow is 670 litres. That includes the amount used for industrial purposes. However, in order to fully satisfy the requirements of the city and the adjoining green belt areas, it has been decided to seek new water supply sources in the Vazuza River (a tributary of the Volga), the Oka River, and the subterranean springs at some distance from the capital. When this project is carried out it will mean a 50% increase in the per capita water consumption of the city.

An extensive transport system is essential for a large city. Moscow's Underground (Metro) went into operation forty years ago. The first line between Sokolniki and Gorky Park was 12 kilometres long. Today the length of the lines is almost 12 times what it was in 1935. When the projected routes are completed, bringing the total length up to 450 kilometres, the Underground will reach practically every part of the city.

The 1930's witnessed the construction of a number of bridges across the Moskva River — the Bolshoi Moskvoretsky, Bolshoi Kamenny, Ustinsky, and Bolshoi Krasnokholmsky. A graceful suspension bridge took the place of the old Krymsky Bridge. Other bridges built at the same time included Maly Moskvoretsky, Kamenny, and Krasnokholmsky on the Vodootvodny Canal, and the Maly Ustinsky and Gospitalny on the Yauza River. The Novoarbatsky Bridge (now Kalininsky) and the double-deck two and a half kilometre Metromost appeared in the 1950's. The plan calls for the construction of 45 more bridges across the Moskva, Yauza and Setun rivers. In addition there are to be more than 150 traffic intersections and over 100 overpasses across railway lines.

Moscow is the biggest railway centre in the USSR with a freight turnover equal to that of Britain, France and Italy taken together. Every day the city's railway stations take care of over a million passengers. Now that the reconstruction of the particularly crowded Kursky Station has been completed the project to modernize the Leningradsky, Kazansky and Paveletsky Stations will soon be launched. A two-storey building extending 160 metres along the railway line will become part of the Byelorussky Station. A station is to go up in the South-West district between the Kievsky and Kaluzhsky highways.

The main river ports such as Severny at Khimki, Zapadny at Fili and Yuzhny at Nagatino handle the grain, vegetables, metal, timber and other goods coming into Moscow and the manufactured articles going out to various parts of the country. Every year 20 million people make use of Moscow's steamship lines. This includes urban and suburban river traffic.

Air lines link the capital with many cities of our vast country and with sixty other countries. New facilities at the Vnukovo, Domodedovo and Sheremetyevo Airports are expected to increase the flow of passengers up to 15 million a year.

Moscow ranks among the finest and cleanest cities in the world. Here is the opinion of Rekiti Minobe, governor of Tokyo: "I was delighted with everything", he said, "— the tree-lined streets, the magnificent ultra-modern buildings of glass and concrete, the monuments of the past, and many other things. As a resident of Tokyo I was particularly impressed with the cleanliness of the air. One can wear a white shirt in Moscow for a whole day, even three days. But in Tokyo the soot from chimney stacks and automobile exhaust fumes instantly turn white into black". On a recent visit to Moscow John Lindsay, Mayor of New York, said that here he could take a deep breath because the air was so fresh and clean.

Special services under Moscow's city and district councils see to it that streets and squares are clean and the air and water reservoirs are free from pollution. Improved methods of city sanitation are constantly being introduced. Engineers are working on vacuum devices that will keep the air virtually dust-free and improve atmospheric conditions in various districts. Large Heating Plants well beyond city limits will take the place of the Heat and Power Stations now functioning in Moscow's central districts. The green belt surrounding Moscow will be expanded to include 275,000 hectares of woodland. Trees to be planted on some 40,000 hectares will form large sections of parkland inside the city.

More of Moscow's inhabitants will be able to enjoy the delights of nature when a year-round health and recreation belt is completed within a radius of 130 to 150 kilometres from the capital.

A part of the belt will extend beyond Moscow Region. Numerous hotels, motels, camping grounds, tourist and sport lodges will accomodate some 6,000,000 people on a summer week-end.

The rhythm of life in Moscow is dynamic. From early morning traffic on the streets is heavy. Electric trains bring in commuters from the suburbs. The smoothly-operating Underground absorbs them and deposits them at their various destinations. The city transport system takes care of 13 million passengers a day. Moscow's industrial life hums with more than 1,600 factories in operation. Their output is exported to 60 different countries.

Work of a different kind goes on at schools, colleges and research institutes. Shops, restaurants and cafés are busy all day long. There are some 20,000 retail trade and public catering establishments in the capital. Construction work is in high gear. We can almost see apartment houses springing up like mushrooms. Pre-fabricated parts are used in putting up thousands of buildings. Construction methods today resemble those of a giant conveyer-belt.

All these municipal activities come under the management of the City and District Councils which make up Moscow's complicated administrative apparatus. Local bodies supervise the work of the city's enterprises, cultural activities, public education, health services, construction of public and residential buildings, improvement projects, trade, communal and transport services.

At the end of the working day the emphasis shifts to entertainment. People flock to cinemas, museums and exhibition halls. The parks, boating areas and stadiums attract those who enjoy more vigorous activities. There's an excited babble of sound at the entrance of the theatres and concert halls. The attendance at Moscow's theatres and cinemas exceeds 153 million a year.

The printing houses work round-the-clock. At newspaper publishing establishments the presses grind out the latest news. The total number of newspapers and periodicals published in Moscow is over 18 thousand million copies a year.

A soft sheen in the sky reflects the lights of the capital at night. Later, when the streets are silent, 7,500 cleaning machines come out to do their job. The Underground maintenance men go down into the tunnels to see that everything is working properly, that the 6,000 trains are ready to operate smoothly and efficiently. Mail trucks can be seen scurrying around town as they make their deliveries at the post offices. The stores too get their supplies of fresh bread, vegetables and other products before daybreak.

In Moscow's new districts the day begins with the singing of birds. These parts of the city blend naturally with the wooded outskirts of Moscow.

We are witnessing the formation of an unusual capital city. It ranks fourth in population, but first in its potentialities. Neither New York, Tokyo or London have the space for our type of planned growth. Further construction could turn them into monster-cities.

Moscow is not threatened with a "high-rise epidemic" which could make a street look like the bottom of a narrow ravine. The average height of Moscow's new buildings has been carefully established and set by the new General Plan.

Moscow's new housing development will incorporate adjacent woodland which will have a tonic effect on the inhabitants. Boulevards will link the city's parks with the embankments of Moskva River also to be planted with trees. In the city's centre the new green areas are to merge with the old parks and squares and form a unified circular park system.

Two more large parks are planned for the capital. One will be laid out in back of Moscow University in the South-West. The other, to be named Victory Park, will be situated on Poklonnaya Hill.

The big new ensembles are planned to harmonize with the cosy nooks redolent of old Moscow. New shades will be added to the light colour scheme peculiar to Moscow's traditional aspect when other republics contribute the best of their own decorative effects.

Express transport lines will connect Moscow's districts with each other, extend to airports and recreation areas, and reach out to the expressways outside the city.

Such is the picture of Moscow as it will be in the near future. Its outlines are already visible like those chiseled in stone by a master craftsman.

Moscow represents something new in city-planning, as it stands on the threshold of a communist civilization as yet unknown to man.

This monument to Lenin in the Kremlin stands in the garden adjacent to Ivanovskaya Square where on May 1, 1920 Lenin took part in the countrywide Communist *subbotnik* (volunteer sparetime work without pay).
Sculptors V. Pinchuk and S. Speransky.

16

In the magnificent modern Palace of Congresses the 22nd, 23rd and 24th Congresses of the Communist Party of the Soviet Union were held.

More than one hundred delegations from Communist and workers', national democratic and socialist parties from various countries attended the 24th Congress. Moscow symbolizes proletarian internationalism and the drive to unify the international communist and workers' movement, to consolidate all the contemporary revolutionary forces.

Leonid Brezhnev, General Secretary of the Central Committee of the CPSU, presented the Central Committee's
Report. The Congress worked out guide-lines for bringing
about a considerable improvement in the well-being of
the people, and endorsed the directives for the Ninth Five-
Year Plan.
The Peace Programme adopted by the Congress met a
warm response in every country; it brought about radical
changes on an international scope easing tensions and
strengthening the feeling of security. The Party's Central
Committee and its Political Bureau are day by day carrying
out practical work to put the Congress decisions into
effect. The efforts of Leonid Brezhnev on behalf of peace
and socialism recently merited the Lenin Peace Prize.

On the eve of the fiftieth anniversary of the establishment of Soviet Power, Moscow was awarded the Order of the October Revolution. Beside the Gold Star and two Orders of Lenin, one more decoration now shines on the banner of the Hero-City.

The Order of the October Revolution was affixed to the banner of Moscow by Nikolai Podgorny, Chairman of the Presidium of the USSR Supreme Soviet.

Moscow is the product of the culture of many generations. Many tales can be told of Borovitsky Hill. Its treasures, created mainly by unknown craftsmen, range from magnificent stone structures on the Kremlin grounds to the unique exhibits at the Armoury.

Any visitor to the Soviet capital goes first of all to Red Square, to the Kremlin. This is the heart of Moscow. Tent-roofed towers rise above its battlements, and beyond them can be seen the golden domes of white stone cathedrals and the silvery roofs of palaces.

In Moscow the new elements have been organically interwoven with those centuries old. Where once there was a maze of narrow streets — the old district of Zaryadye — now stands the giant *Rossia* Hotel, accommodating 6,000. This new architectural ensemble rising above the Moskva River is flanked by priceless specimens of sixteenth and seventeenth-century architecture, which have been carefully restored.

Red Square is always crowded with people.
It was from this square that workers and revolutionary soldiers stormed the Kremlin during the revolutionary days of 1917. From here, too, on a cold, gloomy day, November 7, 1941, men who had been taking part in the anniversary parade left to fight the nazis on a front dangerously near to the capital. And here, at the foot of the Mausoleum, captured fascist banners and standards were flung down in an ignominious heap in June 1945.

Each spring Young Pioneers come here to take a vow to live and work as Lenin did.

This monument erected in 1818 by the sculptor Ivan Martos stands for the greatness and steadfastness of the Russian people. It portrays Kuzma Minin and Dmitry Pozharsky, who at the beginning of the seventeenth century headed a people's volunteer army which drove the Polish and Lithuanian invaders from Moscow.

A guard of honour stands at the entrance to the Lenin Mausoleum day and night. Every hour, at exactly 2 minutes 45 seconds before the hour strikes, a corporal and two guards emerge from the gates of the Spasskaya Tower. They march with measured tread towards the Mausoleum past the blue spruces and terraced stands, past the graves of outstanding revolutionaries and statesmen. In this brief parade of the highest military honour the soldiers take exactly 340 paces. At the instant when they halt at the doors of the Mausoleum the melodious chimes of the Kremlin clock announce that a new hour in the life of the country has started. Then begins the ceremony of the changing of the guard. The corporal quietly gives the command and the newly arrived soldiers take up their posts.

"What powerful, live, noble impressions the Kremlin alone evokes!" The great Russian critic Vissarion Belinsky wrote. "Several centuries have passed over its sacred walls and its tall towers. I cannot fathom the feelings welling up within me on beholding the Kremlin".

The twenty Kremlin towers are incorporated in the high fortress wall which extends over two kilometers.

Five of the towers — Borovitskaya, Vodovzvodnaya, Spasskaya, Nikolskaya and Troitskaya — are crowned with lustrous ruby stars which have come to symbolize the new Moscow.

The Cathedral of the Dormition is simple and austere in its architecture. This is the main building in Cathedral Square on the grounds of the Moscow Kremlin. Organically linked with the surrounding buildings, it is distinguished by its monumental quality. Its elegant body, crowned by five cupolas, is magnificent. The walls are built of white stone blocks and there are two rows of narrow windows high above the ground. Here harmonic unity of external form is combined with a splendid interior. Within, the Cathedral is huge, light and spacious. The internal walls and columns are covered with painting. In the lowest range of the five-tier iconostasis and on additional shelves are paintings dating back to between the eleventh and seventeenth centuries. The renowned eleventh-century icon of St George shows a powerful, courageous man, in whom the medieval artist embodied the people's ideal of military valour. Logically enough, the horseman with a lance, his steed trampling the dragon underfoot, became the ancient emblem of Moscow, which was chased upon the old kopeck piece.

The architectural and decorative elements of the Dormition Cathedral are picturesque, elegant and harmonious in form. There is some superb cast-iron work. The floral lattice grilles, linked by figured uprights, are obviously the work of highly skilled craftsmen. The interesting old frescoes are painted in light, delicate tones and in artistic perfection are close to the works of the outstanding painter Dionysius.

This golden-domed church is superb, its wall-painting is magnificent, and it has priceless icons by Theophanes the Greek, Andrei Rublev and Prokhor of Gorodets. The work of Theophanes the Greek — in the main of a monumental character — is austere. Andrei Rublev's painting has greater warmth and feeling, while in the icons of Prokhor of Gorodets there is a great deal of dramatic intensity.

The Kremlin Cathedral of the Annunciation traces its history back to 1397. Its interior decorations are the oldest in the Kremlin and the most skilful in artistic execution.

Presented here is an outstanding example of early painting — the icon of the Archangel Michael, the work of
Moscow artists at the end of the fourteenth and beginning
of the fifteenth century.

In addition to the cathedrals, at various times palace churches were built in the Kremlin. When the Cathedral of the Annunciation was built craftsmen from Pskov also erected the small, single-domed Church of the Deposition of the Robe (1484-1486). It is a graceful building.

In 1635 and 1636 the Russian architects Bazhen Ogurtsov, Antip Konstantinov, Trefil Sharutin and Larion Ushakov built the Terem Palace, the façade of which is decorated with white-stone window surrounds and portals. Cornices at each storey, and the parapets of the terraces have many other decorative details.

The Faceted Palace is one of the oldest secular buildings in Moscow, having been built in 1487-1491 by the architects Marco Ruffo and Pietro Antonio Solari for official ceremonies and state receptions. From the faceted white stone of the façade comes the name of the building.

The Ivan the Great Bell-tower, the compositional hub of the entire Kremlin ensemble, is among the finest monuments of world architecture. Its history goes back to the time of Ivan Kalita (d. 1340). In 1600, in the reign of Boris Godunov, the bell-tower was added to and crowned with a gilded dome. In the bell-tower and the belfry 21 bells, cast by the master craftsmen Zavyalov, Rusinov, Andrei Chokhov and Ivan Motorin, have survived. The biggest weighs 64 tons. At the foot of the Ivan the Great Bell-tower stands the famous Tsar Bell which weighs more than 200 tons. This was cast in 1733-1735 by Ivan and Mikhail Motorin.

The Kremlin Armoury. Although the State Armoury was built in 1844-1851, in fact this old Russian museum was founded much earlier, at the beginning of the fourteenth century. The Armoury is a repository of fabulous wealth. In it there is the collection of early cold steel, firearms and ammunition: helmets, bows, quivers, arrows, sabres, swords, rifles, pistols, shields, chainmail and other armour. Some coats of chainmail are made of 60,000 fine rings and weigh up to 17 kilograms, while a cuirass may weigh up to ten kilograms. Altogether more than 40,000 weapons and pieces of armour are preserved here.

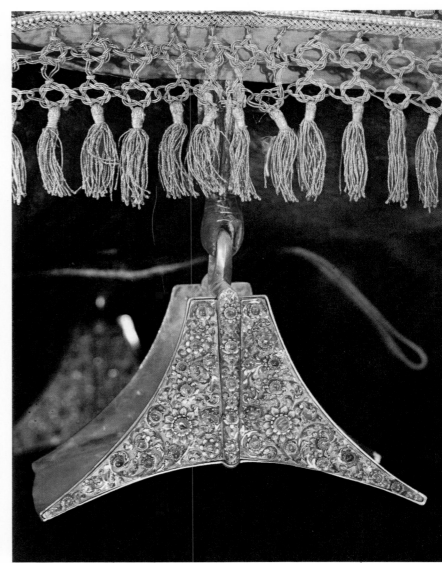

Back in the time of the Grand Princes, and later under the Tsars, priceless treasures were accumulated in the repositories of the Kremlin. The wills of the Moscow Prince Ivan Kalita (d. 1340) and his successors list inherited valuables forming the basis of the royal treasury: icons, vessels, weapons, armour and clothing. As the years went by the treasury was added to by gifts from foreign states and the works of Russian artists and craftsmen.

Bowshafts, sledges, carved and painted window surrounds, shutters, gates, loving cups, salt cellars, distaffs, tables, benches, and wooden buildings constructed without the aid of nails — all these are genuine relics of folk art. What sparkling talent and ingenuity there is in the wonderful lace, the fine embroidery and the work done by Russian armourers, stone and metal carvers, leatherworkers, gold and silversmiths...

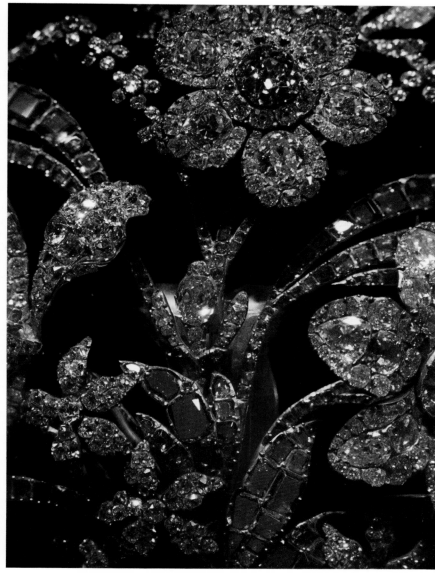

The Armoury was not only a repository but also a workshop, which in the seventeenth century became a centre of Russian artistic handicrafts. Here worked the finest Russian armourers, Nikita Davydov and the Vyatkins, jewellers, silversmiths and enamellers — Gavrila Ovdokimov, Ivan Popov, Danila Osipov, Terentyev and Vassiliev, and the icon-painters Fyodor Zubov, Simon Ushakov and many others from Vladimir, Suzdal, Kostroma and Novgorod...

The Armoury is the repository for highly valuable articles made of gold, silver and diamonds or other precious stones. Dippers, cups, vases, church plate, icon mountings, table clocks and pocket watches are outstanding in their beauty and originality. Here, too, is a collection of fabrics and clothing.

In the mid-sixteenth century Rus was on the upsurge and at this time one of the greatest miracles of world art came into being — the inimitable St Basil's Cathedral, formerly the Cathedral of the Intercession on the Moat. It was built in 1554-1560 in honour of the final liberation of the Russian state from Tartar dependency. The creators of this remarkable work were the legendary architects Posnik Yakovlev and Barma. St Basil's Cathedral is the only one of its kind, a unique artistic monument. In its concept and forms the Cathedral is similar to the Kremlin architecture. Advantageously situated in the very centre of the city, it is a monument to the glory of Russian arms, to the inimitable beauty of early Russian architecture.

The multicoloured cupolas of St Basil's Cathedral reflect the festive, joyful feelings evoked by one of the greatest victories in the history of ancient Rus. St Basil's is a veritable legend in stone — as are the early buildings on Borovitsky Hill, which have provided inspiration for many masterpieces of Russian architecture. Borovitsky Hill, the site chosen on the Moskva River for the fortified Kremlin centuries ago, is now the heart of the capital.

The History Museum and the Lenin Museum stand near
the Kremlin walls, at the opposite end of Red Square from
St Basil's Cathedral. They house many interesting relics
from the eventful history of the Russian people. The
Lenin Museum symbolizes the beginning of a new era in
the life of old Moscow.

Today there is always an endless stream of people passing through Red Square — they come from all over the world to visit the Lenin Mausoleum... They walk slowly past the grave of the Unknown Soldier on which, like a living heart, flutters the Eternal Fire. This is a memorial to the glory of a people who defeated fascism in the most formidable of all wars known to history.

The Eternal Fire on the grave of the Unknown Soldier in
the Alexandrov Gardens, by the Kremlin wall.
The feats of the Soviet people in the Second World War
will be remembered for ever.

War came to each home, to each family. The most bitter, the greatest battle of all those known to mankind, the battle against fascism, began.

The city was girdled with fortifications. The factories were transformed into a mighty arsenal for the front. The first to go over to war production were the *Vladimir Ilyich* Factory, the *Dynamo, Kalibr, Frezer, Krasny Proletary,* and the Motor Works. Thousands of Muscovites worked a double shift.

The State Defence Committee was headed by Joseph Stalin.

The city's appearance changed completely. Hastily printed sign-boards with the inscription "Air-raid shelter" were put up on houses. In parks, public gardens and squares barrage balloons made their appearance, shop windows were obscured by heaps of sandbags, and house windows were criss-crossed with strips of paper. Civil defence squads were formed at factories, offices and schools, and in blocks of flats.

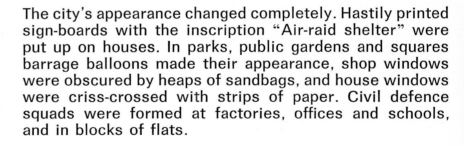

In the battles at the approaches to Moscow Victor Tala-
likhin, Alexei Katrich, Boris Kovzan, Konstantin Titenkov,
Ivan Kholodov and other fighter pilots won renown for
ramming nazi planes.
One October night in 1941 Soviet fighters destroyed 47
enemy bombers.
Moscow had an excellent anti-aircraft defence. In November the enemy made 41 raids on the capital but of 2,000
planes only 28 were able to break through to the city.
Altogether, the anti-aircraft troops defending Moscow
brought down 1,305 planes. The city's defenders displayed
mass heroism.

In the first 45 days of the war 12 divisions of civilian volunteers numbering 120,000 men, almost half of them Communists or Komsomol members, were formed in Moscow under the leadership of the City Party organisation. A total of 42,000 people joined the anti-aircraft troops and air raid defence battalions. Peaceful-minded men and women had to get down to an urgent study of military science. Muscovites learned to deal with the consequences of enemy raids, and to give first aid to their victims. Women and teenagers went to the factories to work the machines left by men who had gone to the front.

On November 6, 1941, a solemn meeting was held in the *Mayakovskaya* Metro Station to mark the 24th anniversary of the Great October Socialist Revolution. The next day the historic parade of troops was held on the snow-blanketed Red Square. From here the defenders of Moscow went off to take up their front-line positions. Even in the most critical days the working rhythm of the city did not flag, all its efforts being directed to defeating the enemy. The working people of the region donated 220 million roubles from their savings for the building of tanks and aircraft.

The great battle of Moscow began. Every hour cost hundreds and thousands of lives. But the troops were determined to stand firm, and not to let the enemy into the capital. The soldiers and officers of the 316th rifle division, commanded by Major-General Panfilov, displayed mass heroism and self-sacrifice. At Dubosekovo, 28 Panfilov heroes stood up to an attack by 50 enemy tanks. They all fell in battle but they did not retreat. In the enemy rear the partisans gave the fascists no peace — the earth burned beneath the invaders' feet. The heroic actions of Zoya Kosmodemyanskaya and many other fearless patriots are immortal.

At the beginning of December 1941, Soviet troops began the counterattack on all sectors of the Moscow defences.

The great battle at the approaches to Moscow culminated in the defeat of the nazi troops. During the fighting 38 fascist divisions were smashed, including 11 tank divisions, 4 motorised and 23 infantry divisions, while the remaining divisions of the "Centre" armies suffered heavy losses. Of the four enemy tank armies operating on the Soviet-German front, 3 were smashed. The fascists lost nearly half a million soldiers and officers, six armies losing 80 per cent of their artillery, tanks and motor transport.

The historic victory was ensured by unparalleled heroism on the part of the Soviet people. At Moscow the nazis suffered their first major defeat in the Second World War. The myth that the German Army was invincible was shattered.

The battles for Moscow were followed by the battles for Stalingrad and Kursk, in the Ukraine and the Crimea, Byelorussia and the Baltic area, around Leningrad and Odessa... Backed by the support of the people in the occupied countries the Red Army drove the fascist invaders out of Poland, Czechoslovakia, Yugoslavia, Bulgaria, Romania, Hungary, Austria and Northern Norway.

Military operations were transferred to the territory of Germany itself.

The names of outstanding military leaders — Marshals of the Soviet Union Ivan Konev, Alexander Vassilevsky, Georgy Zhukov, Konstantin Rokossovsky, Kirill Meretskov, Fyodor Tolbukhin, Rodion Malinovsky, Leonid Govorov, Andrei Yeryomenko, Ivan Bagramyan and others, have gone down in the history of the Second World War.

76

At 5 a.m. on April 16, 1945, more than 40,000 guns and mortars, and over 6,000 tanks and self-propelled guns began hammering at the German capital: several thousand planes swept over Berlin. A total of 140 powerful searchlights dazzled the enemy and lit up the path to the Soviet units. On May 2, 1945, the capital of the German Reich, the sinister nest of fascism in Europe, fell.

On May 8, in the building of the former military engineering college in Karlhorst, a Berlin suburb, representatives of the German High Command signed the act of unconditional surrender of Hitler's Germany. On May 9, Soviet troops carried out their last operation destroying the nazi grouping surrounding Prague, the capital of Czechoslovakia.
The victorious conclusion of the war in Europe was a great cause for rejoicing all over the world.

On June 24, 1945, the Victory Parade was held in Red Square. The finest soldiers of the victorious Soviet Army, decorated with the Gold Stars of Heroes of the Soviet Union and military orders marched through the square. At the foot of the Mausoleum they flung nazi standards.

In Potsdam near Berlin, from July 17 to August 2 there took place a conference of heads of governments of the USSR, USA, and Britain. It adopted a number of decisions designed to ensure a lasting and just peace after the war, and to speed up the trial of the principal nazi war criminals in Nuremberg. They were tried by a court of the nations.

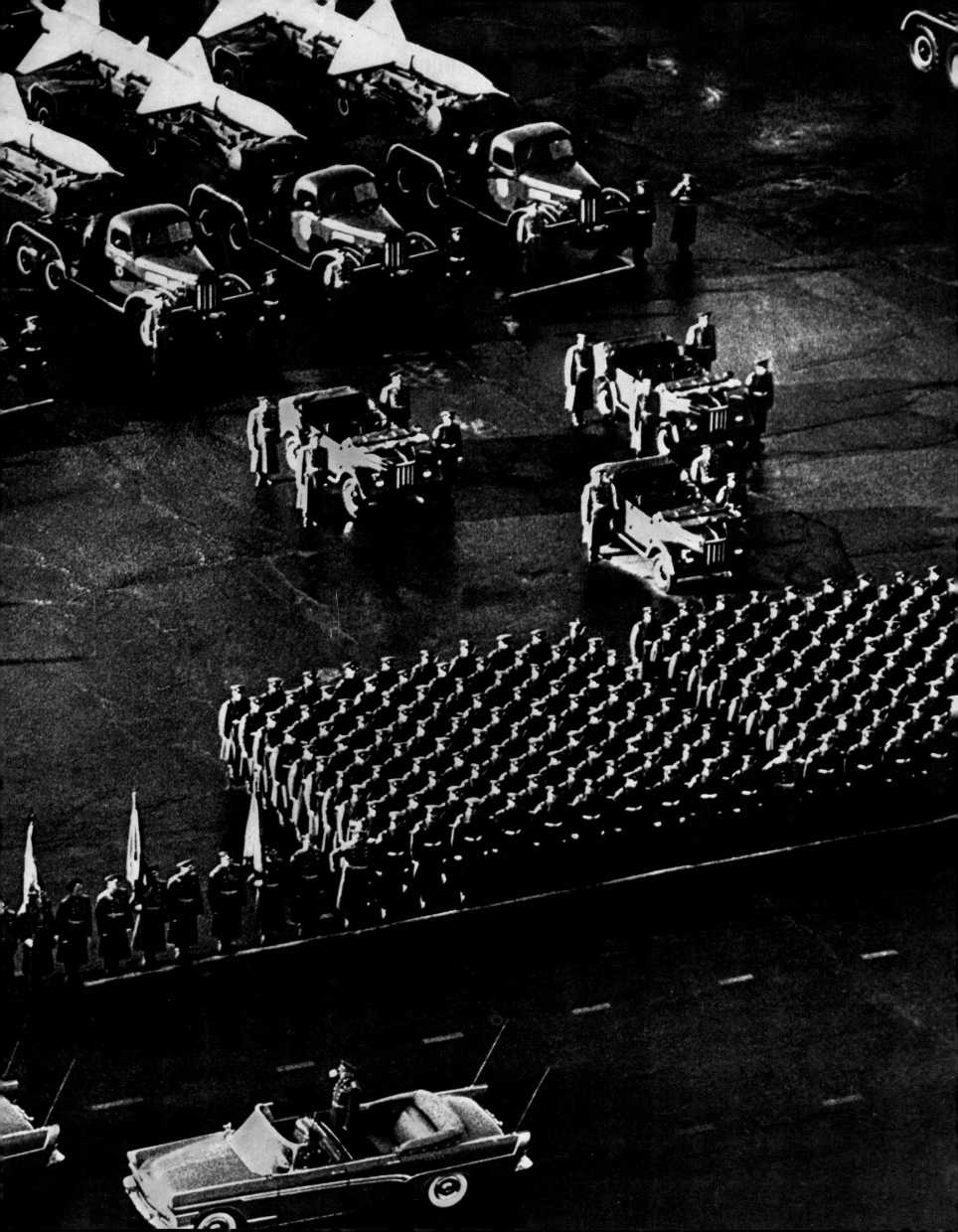

The Peace Programme adopted by the 24th Congress of the Soviet Communist Party calls for utmost effort to get rid of the threat of thermonuclear war, to ease tensions and to achieve peaceful coexistence among nations with different social systems.

The Soviet Union works consistently for peace. It displays initiative and persistence in its efforts to achieve international agreements on the non-proliferation and banning of nuclear weapons, opposes an arms race in strategic weapons, and advocates full and complete disarmament. The specific programme for achieving European security worked out by the Warsaw Treaty states has the aim of stabilising borders and ensuring peaceful co-operation among the states of Europe.

The Soviet Union has put forward an idea of creating a collective security system in Asia.

Under the banner of peace and freedom Moscow welcomes people who come from all over the world to take part in international forums and conferences. The World Peace Congress, which took place in Moscow in October 25—31, 1973, was an outstanding event in the history of the peace movement.

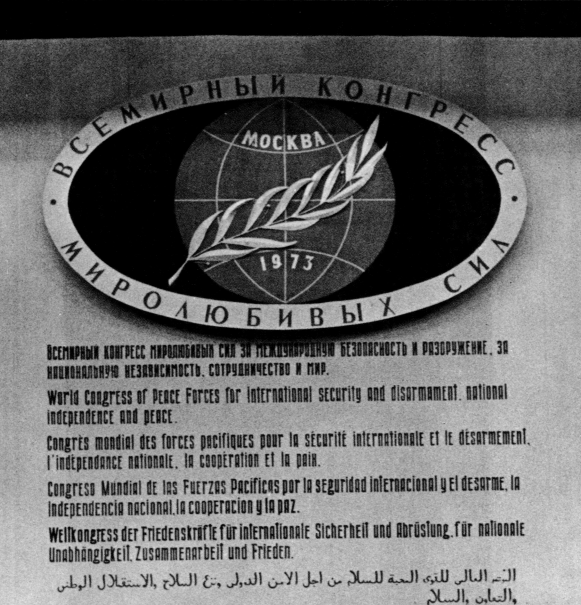

Over 20 million Soviet citizens lost their lives in the war against fascism. Our people, who know what war means, are earnestly striving for peace with its conditions for creative endeavour. In Moscow alone more than 1,200,000 flats were built in the past ten years.

The road from Leningrad. Moscow can be seen across the river.

88

Building is one of the most widespread and honoured occupations in Moscow. In recent years factories which produce large construction elements — whole flats — have gone into operation: in three days a new floor is added to a block, in three months a whole block goes up. To achieve this a "conveyer line" of factories had to be set up to produce prefabricated concrete elements, pressboard, metal details and other components for the building industry. New districts that have been built are sizeable towns in themselves, with 150-200 thousand residents.

89

Once upon a time more than 350 studios and offices were involved in the designing of homes in Moscow and all the amenity buildings that go with them. These tiny organisations were responsible to a variety of departments and ministries. In these circumstances it was impossible to think of industrialising the designing of standard plans. Today designing has been put on a strictly scientific basis and is done only by the biggest architectural studios coming under the Moscow Soviet.

The building workers bring the architects' efforts to fruition. Wherever you look in Moscow you see construction cranes working on new buildings.

Under socialism the supreme aim of social production is the fullest satisfaction of man's material and cultural requirements. More and more housing is being built all the time, and large sums are allocated for municipal services and amenity buildings. Work is proceeding at a tremendous scope. Even greater prospects are opened up by Moscow's General Development Plan.

The city has a staff of highly qualified engineers and architects, large, well-equipped building organisations and a developed building materials industry. But Moscow's transformation into a model Communist city is not a matter solely for the building workers. The USSR Arts Academy has taken the initiative of setting up an Arts Council for the Synthesis of the Arts in Modern Urban Development. Its aim is to unite the efforts of architects, sculptors, painters and experts in the decorative arts in the realisation of the new plan for the capital's construction.

Moscow's industrial workers produce a wide variety of machine tools and instruments, electric motors, transformers, ball-bearings, electronic equipment, footwear, clothing, etc.

Technological progress in industry today means above all greater speeds, pressures, voltages and automatic lines, which increase productivity many times over and free man from heavy physical labour. New technologies require new materials, higher qualifications. The majority of skilled workers at Moscow's enterprises today have complete secondary (ten year) or even higher education. The border between mental and manual labour is being eliminated.

"The working class has been and remains the main productive force in society. Its revolutionary spirit, discipline, organisation and collectivism determine its leading position in the system of socialist relations", Leonid Brezhnev said at the 24th Congress of the CPSU.

Maria Ivannikova, Hero of Socialist Labour and a member of the Central Committee of the CPSU, works at the *Frunze* Cotton Mills in Moscow. She is the initiator of an anti-waste movement, and among her followers are not only textile workers but also metal-workers and workers in the footwear industry and in power engineering.

At the *Orjonikidze* Machine-Tool Building Plant, people speak with pride of Vladimir Komarov, an assembly fitter who holds the title of Hero of Socialist Labour and was a delegate to the 24th Congress of the CPSU. He is a man with a superb command of his job, and even the plant's designers consult him. He willingly passes on the benefit of his vast experience to young workers.

Moscow is the centre for the most advanced work in the field of science and engineering, space exploration, industry and housing construction; Moscow is where efforts are concentrated to penetrate the secrets of the atom and the living cell.

From elementary mathematical, physical and chemical formulas to the most intricate ones stretches the single great chain of modern technical knowledge which is necessary not only to highly qualified specialists but to rank-and-file workers and technicians.

"Today", Mstislav Keldysh, President of the USSR Academy of Sciences said, "as far as the development of production is concerned, it is not necessarily the country that makes the scientific discovery that may prove to be in the lead but the country which is better able to organise the application of this discovery. But the highest level of technological progress will be achieved in the country which attains greater success along the whole front of scientific research". The modern front of scientific research embraces automation and electrification of production processes, the extensive use of atomic energy for peaceful ends, the introduction of electronics and polymers, the exploration of space, and new discoveries in mathematics, physics, chemistry, medicine, genetics and radio-astronomy.

We live in an age of vigorous scientific and technological progress. Science is invading all spheres of life. The creative process has become a collective one, involving workers who devise improvements on the job and designer-inventors, students and leading scientists. Academicians Mstislav Keldysh, Nikolai Semyonov (under whose leadership the complex chemical mechanism of a great number of chain and radial reactions was discovered), and the celebrated mathematician Andrei Kolmogorov are, of course, tackling rather more complicated problems than the average Moscow schoolgirl — but she has everything before her. Considerable attention is being paid to her scientific education, logical in a country which, having wiped out illiteracy, is working constantly on the major scientific problems of the age.

Computers now relieve man of a tremendous amount of work that formerly took up much time and energy that might have been devoted to creative effort. Machines now control automatic installations, sticking strictly to the set regime, they take the place of thousands of book-keeping and accountancy staff, they programme the production flow.

The Soviet people are building atomic power stations, making revolutionary discoveries in experimental and theoretical physics. Our Soviet society offers the greatest opportunities for development and creative work in every field.

Civil aviation has become the most popular form of transport. From Moscow planes fly regularly to 65 states in Europe, Asia, Africa and America. In 1923 a total of 229 passengers and about 2 tons of post and cargo were transported by air; today the same number of passengers can be carried on a single flight made by the inter-continental jet liner, the *IL*-62. Credit for the fine reputation won by Soviet aircraft designing is due to such outstanding scientists and designers as Nikolai Zhukovsky, Sergei Chaplygin, Andrei Tupolev, Nikolai Polikarpov, Sergei Ilyushin, Artem Mikoyan, Semyon Lavochkin and Alexander Yakovlev. Andrei Tupolev, thrice Hero of Socialist Labour and winner of Lenin and State prizes, created the first-ever jet passenger airliner to go into regular service — the *TU*-104. At his design bureau the world's first supersonic passenger plane, the *TU*-144, was designed. A new jet liner, the *TU*-154, has gone into regular service on Aeroflot routes. This plane has a speed of 950 km per hour, and a flight range of 5,500 km; it can carry 164 passengers. Its highly perfected navigational and piloting equipment enables it not only to effect the automatic piloting during flight, but to prepare automatically for landing.

Yury Gagarin, the world's first cosmonaut, and Sergei Korolev, the outstanding Soviet designer, were close friends. The rocket designed by Academician Sergei Korolev launched the artificial Earth sputniks, delivered the USSR emblem to the Moon, made the flight round the Moon when its reverse side was photographed, and carried man into space.

These photographs were taken at Yury Gagarin's home in March 1968, at the last interview given by the pioneer hero of space.

Not far from Moscow is Zvezdny Gorodok (Stellar Town), where the Soviet cosmonauts live and work.

Andrian Nikolayev and Vitaly Sevastyanov were the first to demonstrate the possibility of prolonged space flight, spending 18 days aboard the spaceship *Soyuz-9*.

Valentina Nikolayeva-Tereshkova, Hero of the Soviet Union, is the only woman who has been up into space. "When you think of the place of women in socialist society", said Valentina Nikolayeva-Tereshkova, Pilot-Cosmonaut of the USSR and President of the Soviet Women's Committee, "a society where the principle of equality is not only laid down constitutionally, legally, but is guaranteed by our whole way of life, you realise that such achievements are possible only under socialism".

It was Alexei Leonov who was the first to step out into open space. Only superb training enabled him to cope brilliantly with his tasks in space.

New Moscow silhouettes. Vera Mukhina's famous sculptural group *Worker and Collective Farm Girl,* which surmounted the Soviet pavilion at the Paris World Fair, now stands at the entrance to the USSR Economic Achievements Exhibition, an ensemble of pavilions in a pleasant setting of walks and gardens.

Outside the Exhibition, soaring skywards, is a titanium obelisk erected in honour of the pioneer explorers of space.

Signs of modern Moscow are Moscow
University, the viewing platform of
Moscow University, from which a magnificent panorama of the city opens
up: the graceful arches of the bridges,
the gentle curves of the river in a setting of light stone, and the faceted
spires of tall buildings gleaming in the
sunshine, the Young Pioneers' Palace,
the Metromost, the embankment of the
Gorky Park, and the Luzhniki Stadium...

Moscow has developed according to a historically formed pattern — its radial thoroughfares connected by a complex tangle of old streets, in which are many interesting ancient monuments. A modern block of flats towering over a little church built centuries ago — this is a typical architectural feature of the capital today especially in the older parts of the city.

Once upon a time, along such old streets as Ilyinka (now Kuibyshev Street) and Myasnitskaya (now Kirov Street) the trade routes of the Moscow Principality passed on their way from the Kremlin.

117

Moscow is one of the four biggest cities in the world. In 1917, 1,854,000 people lived here, in 1939 the figure was 4,542,000, while today the capital has more than 7 million residents. People of more than 100 nationalities of the Soviet country live in the capital. The capital has more than 5,000 avenues, streets, squares and lanes. There are giant streets and baby ones: Lenin Avenue, for example, stretches for 14 kilometres, while the length of Venetsianov Street is less than 50 metres.

After the Revolution of 1917 the new city authorities took over the former house of Moscow's Governor-General, a building erected by the well-known architect Matvei Kazakov. The new occupants were the collective governor of the capital — the Moscow Soviet of Working People's Deputies. Its boards, commissions, enterprises, architectural studios and large building trusts run the city's services and ensure the uninterrupted development of the new Moscow. Helping to keep the services of the Moscow Soviet going today are 13 computer centres. In the near future the number of automatic management systems is to increase considerably.

Attractive features of Sovietsky Square, where the Moscow Soviet building stands, Pushkin Square and other squares in the city are the fountains.

This widely known monument to Pushkin was erected in 1880 (sculptor Alexander Opekushin). At the foot of it there are always fresh flowers, an expression of undying affection of the people for Russia's greatest poet. Pushkin and Russia are inseparable in their minds.

The Moscow Underground is the most convenient in the world. An excellent ventilation system provides fresh air and an even temperature the year round. The spacious underground passages and platforms are brightly lighted and decorated with granite, black labradorite, polished oak and walnut, ceramics and plate glass, as well as marble which comes from the Caucasus, the Crimea, the Ural Mountains and Central Asia. Every station is a remarkable example of beauty and elegance.

Unique architectural design and construction have been combined with the finest technical equipment. Automation and electronic techniques make this highly popular mode of travel both fast and reliable.

The Moscow Underground transports some 2 billion people a year. Moscow's underground construction methods have been widely used in other Soviet cities as well as in the capitals of other socialist countries.

123

This is only part of Kalinin Prospekt photographed before the
avenue was completed.

In the evenings the neon signs of cafés and restaurants light up — here Muscovites meet friends, celebrate birthdays, wedding anniversaries, the first night of a new play...

Moscow's landmarks — the Metromost, the new Kalinin Prospekt, the Ostankino Television
Tower, the CMEA Building, the
pylons and arcs of the Krimsky
Bridge, the Panorama-Museum
"The Battle of Borodino"...

Each year almost one and a half million passengers pass through Moscow's nine railway terminuses. All the lines of the Moscow railway network have been electrified. Air routes totalling more than 600,000 kilometres link the Soviet capital with all parts of the world. Railway stations and airports in Moscow are places of meeting and parting — the starting place of all long journeys of Muscovites.

Moscow has become a port of five seas.
Through it almost 40 million tons of
cargo passes each year.
The Moskva River, the city's blue belt,
sets off the ancient hills of the capital.

Summer rain makes the town cool and fresh. Rain-washed Moscow looks even more attractive than usual.

Russian ballet is world famous. The well-known Moscow ballerina Praskovya Lebedeva rivalled such European celebrities as Maria Taglioni and Fanny Esler. No sooner had Yekaterina Geltser left the stage of the Bolshoi Theatre than Victorina Kriger, Olga Lepeshinskaya and Marina Semyonova made their appearance. The press of the world hailed Galina Ulanova as "a miracle of our time" and Maya Plisetskaya as "one of the finest stars in world ballet". How can one forget Ulanova's Juliet, her Maria in *Bakhchisarai Fountain,* and her Giselle, or the characters created by Plisetskaya in innumerable ballets from *Swan Lake* by Tchaikovsky, to Prokofiev's *Stone Flower.*

The annals of the Bolshoi Theatre in Moscow go back to 1776. Its original actors, singers and dancers were either foundlings or peasant serfs — talented, untutored performers. From the heart of the people, too, came the first Russian composers; Mikhail Matinsky, Yevstignei Fomin and Daniil Koshkin. The Bolshoi Theatre has also seen on its stage such magnificent performers as Fyodor Chaliapin, Leonid Sobinov, Antonina Nezhdanova, Nadezhda Obukhova, Valeria Barsova, Maxim Mikhailov, Alexander and Grigory Pirogov, Ivan Kozlovsky, Sergei Lemeshev...

In recent years such acknowledged stars as Leokadia Maslennikova, Mark Reizen, Pavel Lisitsian and Ivan Petrov were joined by a new constellation of talented artists: Irina Arkhipova, Galina Oleinichenko, Yevgeny Kibkalo, Vladimir Atlantov, Alexander Vedernikov... With the advent of Soviet power there was a real creative upsurge of opera and ballet at the Bolshoi. The company staged anew more than one hundred classical operas and ballets and about 80 modern ones, in the main by Soviet composers.

Among the latter are the operas: *War and Peace* by Sergei Prokofiev, *The Decembrists* by Yury Shaporin, *The Taming of the Shrew* by Vissarion Shebalin, *October* by Vano Muradeli, *The Unknown Soldier* by Kirill Molchanov, *The Optimistic Tragedy* by Alexander Kholminov, *Katerina Izmailova* by Dmitry

Shostakovich, and the ballets *A Legend of Love* by Arif Melikov, *Asel* by Vladimir Vlasov, and *Spartacus* by Aram Khachaturyan. These have become firmly established in the company's repertoire.

The brilliant composer Modest Moussorgsky, the author of the popular musical dramas *Boris Godunov* and *Khovanshchina,* was a great innovator of operatic music in the nineteenth century. The corresponding figure in ballet was Pyotr Tchaikovsky. His *Swan Lake, The Sleeping Beauty,* and *The Nutcracker* have enriched the world classical repertoire.

Together with them *Romeo and Juliet* and *Cinderella* by Sergei Prokofiev, *The Fountain of Bakhchisarai* and *The Caucasian Captive* by Boris Asafiev. *The Red Flower* by Reinhold Glieré and *Raimonda* by Alexander Glazunov and *Don Quixote* by Ludvig Minkus have triumphed on the stage of the Bolshoi for many years.

Yury Grigorovich's production of Aram Khachaturyan's ballet *Spartacus*, is one of the Bolshoi's finest spectacles.

The heroic theme, despite the complex story, finds vivid expression in the concept of the choreographer, in the extraordinary beauty and sculptural eloquence of the dance.

Spartacus is an invariable success with both Soviet and foreign audiences.

143

Dmitry Shostakovich, the pride of Soviet musical culture, Hero of Socialist Labour, and Lenin and State Prize winner, has been dubbed the composer of the century.

When Svyatoslav Richter plays the piano audiences are enraptured. Behind the perfection of his music are days and nights of agonised thought, constant searchings and new discoveries.

144

Musical and theatrical Moscow is a world of drama and opera theatres, orchestras and dance companies. Deserved popularit is enjoyed by the USSR State Symphony Orchestra, the Osipov Folk Instruments Orchestra, the Alexandrov Red Army Song and Dance Ensemble, the USSR State Folk Dance Ensemble, the Beryozka Dance Ensemble, and the Pyatnitsky Russian Folk Choir.

148

Hundreds of thousands of Muscovites study in their spare time. One in five of the working population has a higher education, and one in three has a specialised secondary education or higher. The capital has more than 4,000 libraries with nearly 300 million volumes. Each year about three million people visit Lenin Library, one of the biggest in the world.

Books are the constant companions of Muscovites. On the proposal of the Soviet Union, UNESCO declared 1972 to be International Book Year, and it was marked here with All-Union and republican exhibitions, fairs, book months and weeks, and readers' conferences.

Mikhail Sholokhov, Hero of Socialist Labour, and the author of *And Quiet Flows the Don, Virgin Soil Upturned* and *Fate of a Man,* is one of the most widely-read authors in the world. His books have been published in dozens of languages and in all countries.

Konstantin Fedin, Hero of Socialist Labour, one of the founders of Soviet literature, is also the author of books on the art of writing, a serious critic and theoretician. He is now Chairman of the Board of the USSR Writers' Union.

The message of Leonid Leonov's books is patriotism, loyalty to an idea and love of mankind. Maxim Gorky urged young people to study the language of this outstanding writer. Leonid Leonov is a Hero of Socialist Labour.

The Pushkin Fine Arts Museum is the repository of cultural treasures of the Ancient Orient, the world of classical antiquity, and of Western Europe. Among its exhibits are objects from Ancient Egypt which are at least 6,000 years old. There are also works of monumental sculpture, Coptic textiles, Fayum portraits, fragments of ancient Greek and Roman architecture, copies of the better-known sculptures of Ancient Greece, the European Renaissance, the ancient Assyrians, the northern coast of the Black Sea.

In the picture gallery are works from the major European schools of art — the Italian, Spanish, Dutch, Flemish, etc. Renaissance art is represented by many works by such artists, as Perugino and Botticelli, the magnificent *St Sebastian* by Boltraffio, and the *Fornarina* by Giulio Romano, Rafael's pupil and assistant. There is a superb collection of works by Rembrandt, Peter Paul Rubens, Anton Van Dyck, Murillo, Lucas Cranach...

154

The Fine Arts Museum possesses a most extensive collection of works by French painters, including works of Nicolas Poussin — a striking representative of seventeenth-century French classicism, of that great French realistic painter Jean Chardin, that master of architectural landscape Hubert Robert, paintings of Louis David, Eugène Delacroix, the Barbizons. The Museum has on view some of the best works of Auguste Renoir, Alfred Sisley, Edgar Degas, Paul Cézanne, Vincent Van Gogh, Paul Gauguin, Henri Matisse and Pablo Picasso.

Perugino. *Madonna and Child.*

Rembrandt. *Portrait of an Old Woman.*
(Possibly it is a portrait of the wife of
Rembrandt's brother).

The State Tretyakov Gallery is without equal among the national art museums of the world. Just as the finest works of Russian progressive literature influenced the development of progressive thought of the day, so did the gallery founded by the well-known Moscow art connoisseur Pavel Tretyakov and presented by him to the state become a source of new ideas and emotions. Nadezhda Krupskaya tells us that Lenin, while in emigration, obtained a catalogue of the Tretyakov Gallery from acquaintances and "would sit engrossed in it".

158

The Tretyakov Gallery has collected all the finest works done by Russian painters of the last two centuries: Alexander Ivanov, Karl Bryullov, Pavel Fedotov, Alexei Venetsianov, Vassily Perov, Ivan Aivazovsky, Ilya Repin, Vassily Surikov, Ivan Kramskoi, Victor Vasnetsov, Vassily Vereshchagin, Valentin Serov, Mikhail Vrubel, Alexei Savrasov, Isaak Levitan, Nikolai Yaroshenko, Isaak Brodsky, Mi-

trofan Grekov, Alexander Gerasimov and Pavel Korin. The Museum has a unique collection of portraits painted by masters of various times: Fyodor Rokotov, Dmitry Levitsky, Vladimir Borovikovsky, Orest Kiprensky, Vassily Tropinin, Vassily Perov, Ivan Kramskoi, Ilya Repin and Valentin Serov.

Valentin Serov. *The Overgrown Pond.*

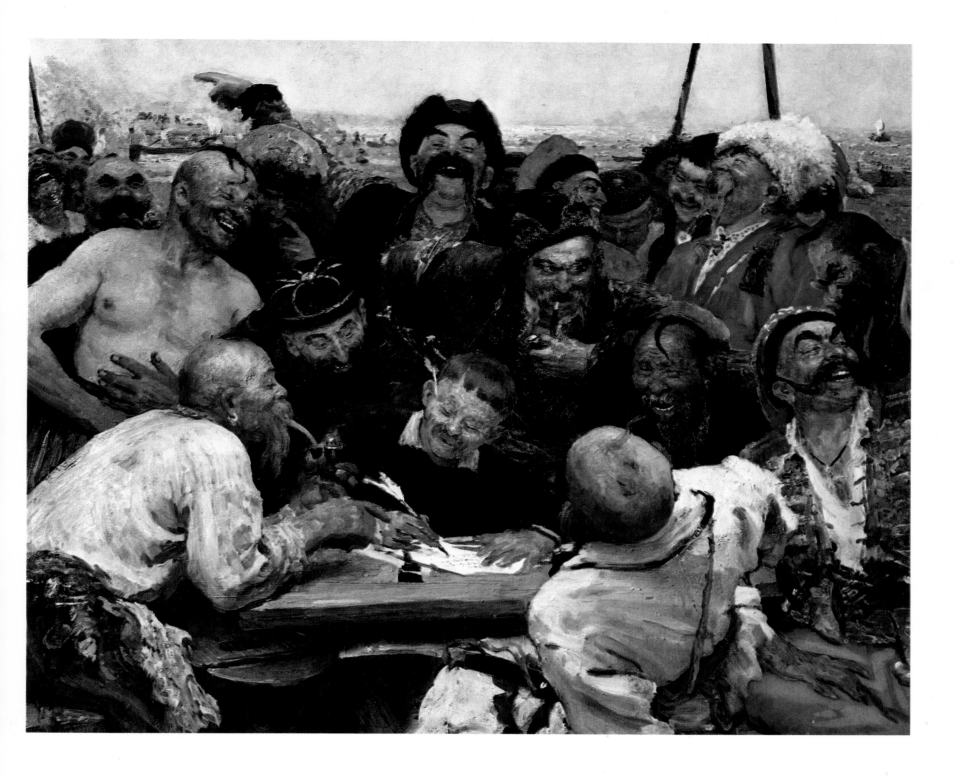

Ilya Repin and Vassily Surikov occupy a special place in Russian representational art. Their work marks the heights of the art of the *peredvizhniks*. It opened a new age in the development not only of Russian but of world painting. In the works of these outstanding painters Russian history was first depicted with forceful realism. The *Zaporozhye Cossacks Write a Letter to the Turkish Sultan* is a study for Repin's famous picture, which is full of witty, biting humour.

Even from these details of works by Vassily Surikov one can get an idea of the painter's great talent. *The Morning of the Execution of the Streltsi* is a vivid expression of the complex and contradictory character of Peter the Great's time. Vladimir Stassov, the famous Russian art critic, described *The Boyarinia Morozova* as the acme of Russian painting.

The Gallery also has a fine collection of Soviet paintings. Here are works by painters of a wide variety of styles and artistic vision: Alexander Deineka, Martiros Saryan, Ilya Mashkov, Kozma Petrov-Vodkin, Georgy Ryazhsky, Fyodor Bogorodsky, Mikhail Nesterov, Pyotr Konchalovsky, Isaak Brodsky, Alexander Gerasimov, Mitrofan Grekov, Georgy Savitsky, Arkady Plastov, Nikolai Romadin, Vladimir Serov, Alexander Laktionov, Sergei Gerasimov, Georgy Nissky, Semyon Chuikov and Vassily Yefanov; the sculptors Ivan Shadr, Vera Mukhina, Nikolai Andreyev, and Sergei Konenkov; the graphic artists Dmitry Moor, Vladimir Favorsky, Yevgeny Kibrik, Boris Prorokov, Dementy Shmarinov, Nikolai Ponomaryov, Georgy Vereisky and Anatoly Yar-Kravchenko... This collection represents all major trends in Soviet fine arts.

Boris Yoganson. *Interrogation of Communists.*

Yury Pimenov. *New Moscow.*

Yevgeny Vuchetich, Hero of Socialist Labour, People's Artist of the USSR, Lenin and State Prize winner, and holder of the Jawaharlal Nehru Prize, is Vice-President of the USSR Academy of Arts. He has done memorial sculptures of Lenin, busts of war heroes, sculptural portraits of workers and collective farmers, scientists, writers, artists, etc. He is the author of the monument to the Soviet Army erected in Berlin and the memorial ensemble on Mamayev Hill commemorating the Battle of Stalingrad.

Semyon Chuikov, People's Artist of the USSR, Academician, State Prize winner. His best-known works are *Kirghiz Collective Farm Suite, A Shepherd's Daughter* and *Girl with a Flower*. For his many works on Indian themes, Chuikov was awarded the Nehru Prize.

167

In the northern part of Moscow, not far from the USSR Economic Achievements Exhibition are ancient oakwoods, which come close to the Ostankino Palace — now the Museum of Serf Art. Once Count Sheremetiev delighted his guests with the beauty of the avenues and ponds of his estate here — today the grounds of Ostankino are a public park.

The Ostankino Palace and grounds offer the visitor a well-preserved complex of old Russian architecture and landscaping prevalent at the end of the eighteenth century. The Palace was built by the gifted Russian architects A. Mironov, G. Dikushin and P. Argunov who were all serfs. Although it's a wooden building it gives the impression of a monumental stone structure. The Museum at Ostankino is the only one in Russia with a collection of lighting devices. It was also known for its fine theatre.

The Kolomenskoye Estate-Museum, a magnificent ensemble of architectural monuments, was once the country residence of the Russian Tsars. The first mention of Kolomenskoye in chronicles goes back to the time of Ivan Kalita who was Moscow's Prince in the fourteenth century. In 1532 the Church of the Ascension was built here, the first stone church with a tent-roof, which is still impressive with the unusual beauty of its architecture. Another splendid piece of architecture is the Church of St John the Baptist, built by Ivan the Terrible in the mid-sixteenth century.

In 1606 Kolomenskoye was used as a camp for the army of Ivan Bolotnikov, the outstanding leader of a peasant uprising. Today Kolomenskoye is part of Moscow.

In addition to ancient monuments, the state takes under its protection river valleys, the banks of reservoirs and landscapes of particular beauty.

As in a fairy-tale birch-bark cradle from whence came folk heroes of old, Moscow is enfolded in its famous birch forests. On all sides of the city stretch meadows, threaded through by small, gently-flowing rivers, copses, woods, and fields. Into this enchanted land one plunges directly on leaving Moscow.

Trees glittering with hoar-frost, a sharp drop to the river, tracks through the snow and air blue with frost. Miracle-working spring is the time of Nature's awakening. And then people wait expectantly for summer, with its hot days, its swimming, the fragrance of hay, honey and apples. Autumn, too, has its own beauty, with its patterns of crimson and gold, the pungent smell of mushrooms and fallen, rain-soaked leaves. But Russians have a special affection for their winter.

Even when the thermometer registers 30° of frost there are plenty of people in Red Square, waiting to enter the Lenin Mausoleum.

The Kremlin in winter. The wind sweeps powdered snow from the domes of the centuries-old churches, and wafts it through the Kremlin's streets and squares. And at the height of winter, when hoar-frost festoons the branches, even stone and metal freeze.

The Tsar Cannon is a noteworthy monument of Russian foundry art. It was made in 1586, and the name of the craftsman who 150 years before the Tsar Bell was cast succeeded in creating this miracle was Andrei Chokhov. The cannon, cast in bronze, weighs 40 tons and is over five metres long.

Midnight Kremlin wrapped in winter's snow,
With Ivan the Great, that belfry tall,
Guarding Moskva River, Moscow city,
With the shadow of your loop-holed wall.
Kremlin, neath the winter moonlight clear,
You are splendid in your hoary past,
And as glorious in the triumphs won so dear,
Whose memories, still fresh, will ever last...
Kremlin in the winter night,
Your walls and loop-holes, domes and towers
With age-old legends shine as bright
As with your recent hard-won glory...
And from your every stone and battlement
There glows incessantly, unseen,
The light of Stalingrad and Leningrad,
And of our banner flying o'er Berlin.
                    ALEXANDER TVARDOVSKY

Red Square in its winter finery. Flood-lights illuminate the granite viewing tiers and the necropolis of the Kremlin wall. Standing like sentinels in the silence are silvery fir trees, keeping guard over the sleep of heroes of the Revolution, those who gave their lives for the power of the Soviets, for the people's happiness.

The stars of the Kremlin which shine at night with the crimson glow of hope, the steeples of the tall buildings which the pilot of an airliner sees from afar on a sunny day, the tower-like structures of the new Kalinin Prospekt, the ribbon of the Moskva River winding its way between the banks of parks and gardens — all this is Moscow.

There is an enchantment about Moscow that makes it unforgettable. We feel it in the early light of dawn and in the deepening twilight, in the sudden summer shower, in the swirling snow of winter. Daybreak on the Moskva River is a memorable sight with the granite of the embankment becoming more silvery as day approaches, and the shape of the bridges emerging gradually from the rosy mist.

200

202

Ordinary, workday Moscow has its
own beauty with its familiar streets, in-
timate little gardens, well-known buildings and monuments...
The traffic lights seem to hang from a
tree, bathing it alternately in a red, am-
ber and green glow.
In the evenings Moscow Conservatory
is a nocturne in which Tchaikovsky's
inspired music can be heard.

At night when the city is ablaze with
light the Kremlin seems to float over it.
Far beyond Moscow's limits one can
see the glow of the illuminations, a
glow that seems to descend upon the
Earth from the mysterious regions of
Space.

YURY BALANENKO, ALEXANDER BEREZIN
MOSCOW

Translated from Russian by
GALINA STRELKOVA, VICTORIA MASLENINA

© Translated from Russian
Planeta Publishers, Moscow 1975

Printed by AMILCARE PIZZI s.p.a. - arti grafiche,
Milan (Italy)